TIP 2 Support your child as he/she reads the story pages:

- give the book to your child to read and turn the pages.

- where necessary, encourage your child to break a word into syllables, sound out each one, and then flow the syllables together. Ask him/her to reread the sentence to check the meaning.

- when there's a question mark or an exclamation mark, encourage your child to vary his/her voice as he/she reads the sentence. Demonstrate how to do this if it is helpful.

TIP 3 Chat at the end of each page:

- ask questions about the text and the meaning of the words used. These help to develop comprehension skills and awareness of the language used.

A FEW ADDITIONAL TIPS

- Always encourage your child to try reading difficult words by themselves. Praise any self-corrections, for example, "I like the way you sounded out that word and then changed the way you said it, to make sense."

- Try to read together everyday. Reading little and often is best. These books are divided into manageable chapters for one reading session. However, after 10 minutes, only keep going if your child wants to read on.

- Read other books of different types to your child just for enjoyment and information.

Series consultant, **Dr. Linda Gambrell**, Distinguished Professor of Education at Clemson University, has served as President of the National Reading Conference, the College Reading Association, and the International Reading Association.

Penguin
Random
House

Project Editor Laura Gilbert
Editors Natalie Edwards, Matt Jones,
Clare Millar
Designer Jon Hall
Senior Slipcase Designer Mark Penfound
Senior Designer David McDonald
Pre-Production Producer Kavita Varma
Producer Isobel Reid
Managing Editor Sadie Smith
Design Managers Guy Harvey,
Ron Stobbart
Creative Manager Sarah Harland
Publisher Julie Ferris
Art Director Lisa Lanzarini
Publishing Director Simon Beecroft

For Lucasfilm
Assistant Editor Samantha Holland
Image Archives Newell Todd,
Gabrielle Levenson
Art Director Troy Alders
Story Group Leland Chee, Pablo Hidalgo,
Matt Martin

Reading Consultant
Linda B. Gambrell, Ph.D

This edition published in 2017
First American Edition, 2007
Published in the United States by DK Publishing
345 Hudson Street, New York, New York 10014
DK, a Division of Penguin Random House LLC

Page design copyright © 2017 Dorling Kindersley Limited

Slipcase UID: 001–309482–Dec/17

A catalog record for this book is available from
the Library of Congress

ISBN: 978-0-7566-3269-4

Printed and bound in China

www.dk.com
www.starwars.com

A WORLD OF IDEAS:
SEE ALL THERE IS TO KNOW

A QUEEN'S DIARY

Written by Simon Beecroft

My name is Padmé Amidala.

I am the Queen of my planet.

Today I am going to start a diary.

I am going to start a diary because my life is very busy.

I do not want to forget anything.

My world

If people read this diary in the future, they might not know about my world. So I am going to explain interesting things about my world in these boxes.

Today I tried to count all the rooms
in the palace, where I live.
I quickly lost count.
My palace is so large I think I shall
never be able to explore all of it.

I love to climb up to one of the highest rooms.
Then I gaze at the waterfalls that flow down the side of the mountain.

Home world

I live on a planet called Naboo.
Naboo is a small planet.
It is very beautiful.

Today a lot of important people
visited me.

When people meet me, some of them
are surprised that I am so young.

I am just 14 years old.

All queens on my planet are young.

I am not even the youngest!

Even though I am not very old,
I want to be a good queen.

Landspeeder

This morning I flew in a landspeeder.
I love travelling fast in landspeeders.
I flew around the city and looked at
all the pretty buildings.
Lots of people waved at me.

My palace is in the biggest city
on Naboo, but I have not always
lived here.
I was born in a mountain village.

People of Naboo
The humans who
live on my planet
are called the Naboo.
I am one of them.
The Naboo live in
cities and villages.

I was learning about the Gungans
in my lessons today.

I learned that the Gungans also
live on my planet.

They live in underwater cities.

The Gungans can also live on land.

I would like to meet a Gungan.

Gungan   *Naboo*

Naboo natives

The Naboo and the Gungans do not often meet each other. They are not enemies, but they are not friends either!

I often think about my
parents and sisters.
I have many memories
of growing up
in my village.

When I was young,
my teachers realized
I was very clever.
My teachers gave me
extra training.
Later, people
decided to vote for
me as Queen.
It was the proudest
day of my life!

Padmé

Ruwee

Sola

Jobal

Eirtaé

Rabé

I have handmaidens who look
after me and help me dress.
They also protect me from danger.

My handmaidens are my friends, too.
Eirtaé (pronounced AIR-TAY)
and Rabé are two of my
closest handmaidens.

Royal dress

On my planet,
kings and queens
wear special clothes
and makeup.
They also wear their
hair in special ways.

Today I am going to visit a nearby planet in my special spaceship. My spaceship is totally silver.

Spaceships

Naboo kings and queens fly silver spaceships. There is even a throne in my ship!

It has large rooms inside.

No one has a spaceship like mine.

I am even learning to fly it.

Sabé

Sometimes it is hard being Queen,
because everyone knows me.
Sabé is my best friend
and one of my handmaidens.

Padmé

Sometimes Sabé dresses as me,
and I dress as a handmaiden.
We have a secret way of talking
in code when we are in disguise.

A terrible thing has happened.
My planet has been invaded.
Enemy soldiers tried to capture me,
but I was saved by two Jedi Knights.
I had never met a Jedi before,
but I had heard about them.
They travel everywhere to help
people in need.

Droid soldiers

The enemy soldiers are machines called droids. Every droid soldier is armed and dangerous.

Now we are flying away from my planet to search for help for my people.

We have landed on a planet
to repair the spaceship.
The planet is rough and dry.
We went to a local town.
I went in disguise so no one
would know I was a queen.
I met a boy who is a slave.
This means that someone
owns him, and he is not free
to ever leave his master.

This young boy is very special.

His name is Anakin.

He told me I looked like an angel.

I think we will be friends.

The Jedi think that
Anakin is special.
They think that he
might have special
powers, like a Jedi.
They want to free
him from slavery,
so he can learn how
to be a Jedi.

Amazing news! Anakin is free!

He won a dangerous race in his

Podracer to gain his freedom.

Now we can get help for my planet.

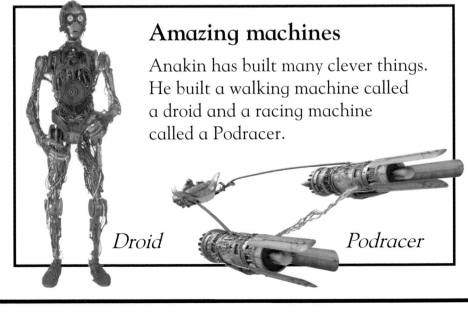

Amazing machines

Anakin has built many clever things.
He built a walking machine called
a droid and a racing machine
called a Podracer.

Droid

Podracer

Today I became a fighter.
No one would help my people,
so I had to help them myself.
I went with the Jedi to ask the
Gungans for help.

Together we made an army
and fought the enemy droid soldiers.
The Gungans fought bravely,
but many of them died.

Weapons

The Gungans use
many weapons in
battle, including
giant catapults.

My planet is free!

Anakin helped us a lot.

He flew a spaceship straight into the invaders' spaceship and blew it up! Although it was really an accident, when Anakin destroyed the ship the droids could no longer fight.

Now I'm sure Anakin will be trained as a Jedi. Perhaps we will meet again....

Places I have visited

I traveled to the swamps on my planet. The Gungans have a secret meeting place there.

I visited a dangerous planet called Tatooine with the Jedi Qui-Gon Jinn. We went to a busy town.

When I was visiting Tatooine, I watched a fast sporting race called a Podrace. A huge crowd gathered to watch the race.

I flew to the center of the galaxy to visit the capital planet. One enormous city covers the entire planet.